GROUNDBREAKER BIOS

Anne Frank

BY HEATHER C. HUDAK

CONTENT CONSULTANT
DR. F. K. SCHOEMAN
ASSOCIATE PROFESSOR
DIRECTOR OF JEWISH STUDIES
UNIVERSITY OF SOUTH CAROLINA

Kids Core
An Imprint of Abdo Publishing
abdobooks.com

abdobooks.com

Published by Abdo Publishing, a division of ABDO, PO Box 398166, Minneapolis, Minnesota 55439.

Printed in the United States of America, North Mankato, Minnesota.
102021
012022

Cover Photo: Anne Frank Fonds Basel/Premium Archive/Getty Images
Interior Photos: Pictorial Press Ltd/Alamy, 4–5, 28 (top); Everett Collection Inc/Alamy, 6; Frank Rumpenhorst/picture-alliance/dpa/AP Images, 8, 28 (bottom); Red Line Editorial, 10; Everett Collection/Shutterstock Images, 12–13; Süddeutsche Zeitung Photo/Alamy, 15; Globe Stock Premium/Alamy, 17, 29 (top); Andreas Arnold/picture alliance/Getty Images, 18, 29 (bottom right); Alpha Historica/Alamy, 20–21; iStockphoto, 22, 24, 29 (bottom left); dpa picture alliance archive/Alamy, 26

Editor: Ann Schwab
Series Designer: Christine Ha

Library of Congress Control Number: 2021941510

Publisher's Cataloging-in-Publication Data

Names: Hudak, Heather C., author.
Title: Anne Frank / by Heather C. Hudak
Description: Minneapolis, Minnesota : Abdo Publishing, 2022 | Series: Groundbreaker bios | Includes online resources and index.
Identifiers: ISBN 9781532196843 (lib. bdg.) | ISBN 9781644946688 (pbk.) | ISBN 9781098218652 (ebook)
Subjects: LCSH: Frank, Anne, 1929-1945--Juvenile literature. | Diarists--Biography--Juvenile literature. | Netherlands--Amsterdam--Juvenile literature. | Jews--Biography--Juvenile literature. | Jewish children in the Holocaust--Biography--Juvenile literature. | Women authors--Biography--Juvenile literature.
Classification: DDC 940.5318092 [B]--dc23

CONTENTS

Anne dreamed of becoming a famous writer or journalist.

CHAPTER 1

Who Was Anne Frank?

On June 12, 1942, Anne Frank turned thirteen. She was thrilled when she received a diary for her birthday. It had a red-and-white checkered cover. She addressed her entries to an imaginary friend named Kitty.

Otto Frank with his daughters, Margot, *left*, and Anne

Anne was a Jewish girl from Germany. She lived at a time when Jews were not seen as equals to other people. Millions were killed for being Jewish. Anne and her family went into hiding to escape. She wrote about these experiences in her diary. It was later published so people could read about her life. Today, Anne is a role model to people everywhere.

Anne's Early Years

Annelies Marie Frank was born on June 12, 1929, in Frankfurt, Germany. She was called Anne for short. Her father, Otto, worked for a bank. Anne's mother, Edith, cared for Anne and her older sister, Margot.

The Frank family home in Frankfurt, Germany

The Frank family was Jewish. Many people in Germany at that time disliked Jews. There were few jobs. Many people did not have enough money. People wrongly blamed Jews for these problems. They also falsely believed that Jews were the reason Germany lost World War I (1914–1918). Anne's family worried for their safety.

What Is Anti-Semitism?

Anti-Semitism is the hatred of Jews as a religious or **ethnic** group. Jews have experienced this hatred for thousands of years.

This map of present-day Germany and the Netherlands shows the three different cities where Anne Frank lived during her early years. How does this map help you understand the changes Anne experienced during that time?

Anne's father moved to Amsterdam, the Netherlands, in 1933. Her mother and Margot arrived later that year. Anne stayed with her grandmother in Aachen, Germany. She joined her family in February 1934.

Further Evidence

Look at the website below. Does it give any new evidence to support Chapter One?

The Complete Works of Anne Frank

abdocorelibrary.com/anne-frank

Adolf Hitler was the leader of the Nazi Party.

CHAPTER 2

No Longer Safe

The **Nazi Party** took control of Germany in 1933. It hated Jewish people. The Nazis' leader was Adolf Hitler. He wanted to control the world. He also wanted to rid it of all Jews.

After leaving Germany, Anne's father found a good job in Amsterdam. Life for Anne's family was very good for a while. Anne liked her new home and school. She was smart, outgoing, and had many friends.

On September 1, 1939, World War II (1939–1945) began. The Nazis invaded the Netherlands on May 10, 1940. The Nazis made life hard for Jewish people. Jews could no longer own property or use public transportation. The Nazis destroyed **synagogues** and Jewish-owned shops. Jews lost most of their **rights**.

The Nazis built different types of camps where they kept Jews and other prisoners of war. The prisoners were treated horribly.

As a budding author, Anne wrote short stories and even began working on a novel.

They were forced to work in poor conditions. They did not have enough food or clothing. The camps were unclean, and many people became ill or died. The Nazis also sent Jews to these camps to be killed.

The Secret Annex

On July 5, 1942, Margot received a written order to work at a camp. Anne's father had already begun making a secret hiding place for the family. It was in the **annex** of his office building. They moved there the next day. Soon, four more people joined them.

Eight people living in such a small space was not easy. They had to be very quiet, especially

The Holocaust

In 1941, Hitler decided to wipe out all Jews. This time in history is known as the Holocaust. The Nazis hurt and murdered Jews. They killed about 6 million Jews before the end of World War II. About 1.5 million Jewish children were killed.

Eight people hid from the Nazis in the secret annex.

during the day. They did not want the workers downstairs to hear them. They had to be careful that people in the buildings nearby didn't see them. Only a few trusted people knew where they were.

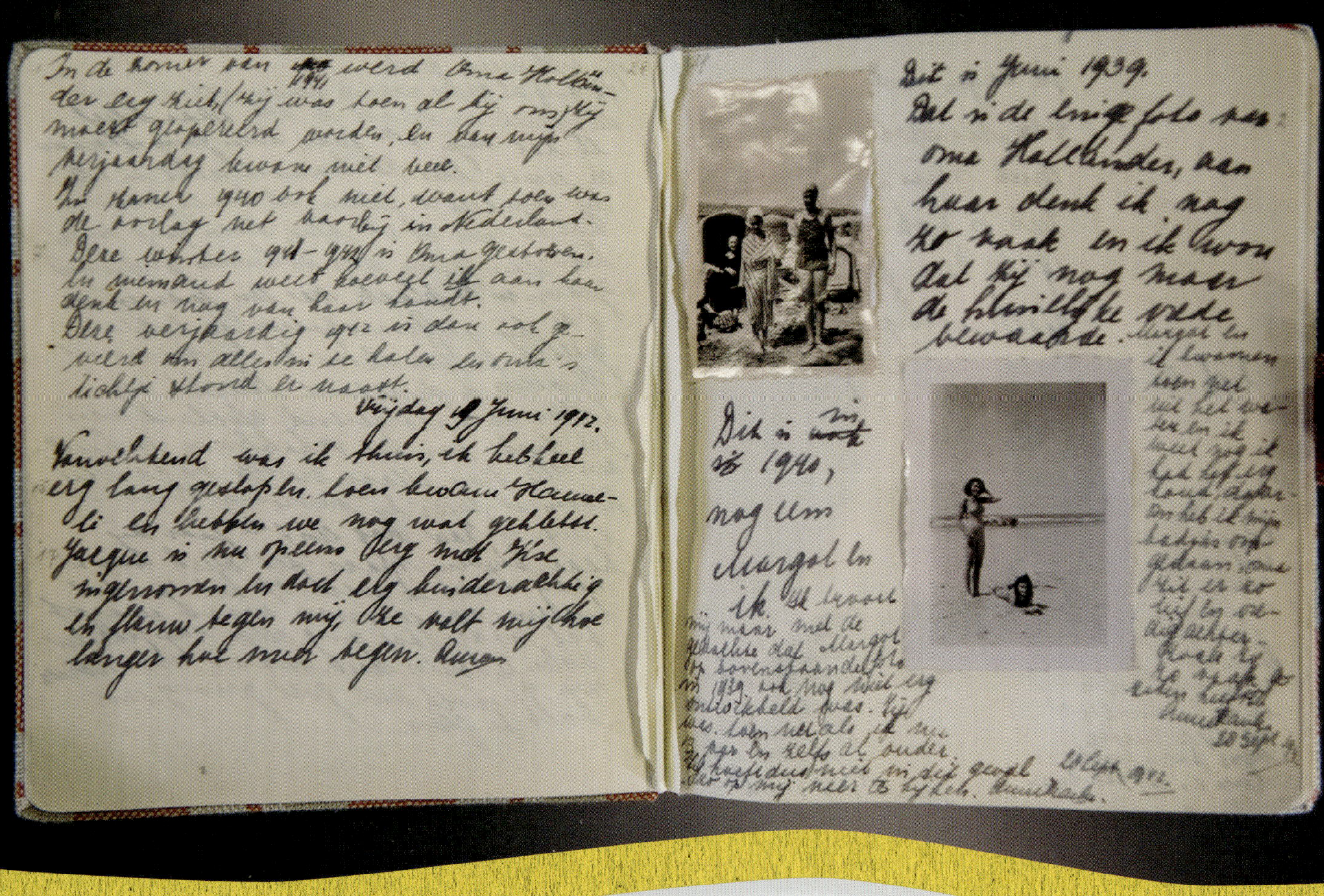

Along with Anne's private thoughts, her diary included vacation photos taken during happier times.

These helpers brought them food and other supplies. They risked their lives to help Anne and the others. It was against the law to help Jews. Anne wrote in her diary about her feelings, life in the annex, and the war.

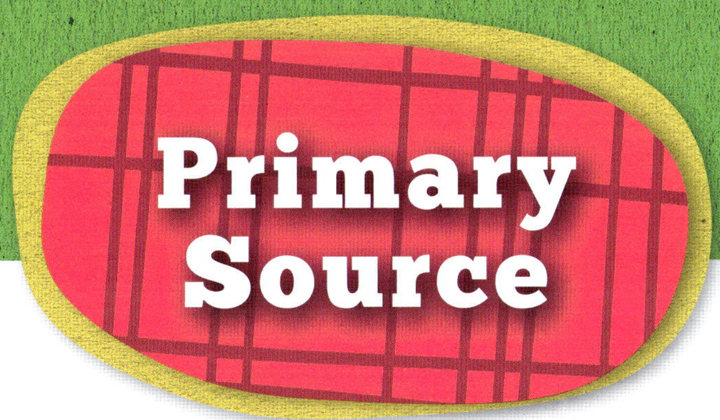

Author Elie Wiesel survived the Nazi camps at Auschwitz and Buchenwald during World War II. During an interview, he said this about his experience:

> When you've actually experienced it, every cell of your being is different. What we lived through is beyond language.

Source: Oprah Winfrey. "Oprah Talks to Elie Wiesel." *O, the Oprah Magazine*, Nov. 2000, oprah.com. Accessed 27 July 2021.

Point of View

What is the author's point of view on this topic? What is your point of view? Write a short essay about how they are similar and different.

The Nazis capture Jews living in Warsaw, Poland. The Nazis forced millions of European Jews from their homes. Most did not survive the Holocaust.

CHAPTER 3

The Secret Is Out

On August 4, 1944, Nazi SS men raided the secret annex. The SS were a special Nazi police force. All eight people inside the annex and two of their helpers were arrested.

They had lived in constant fear of this moment for 761 days.

A memorial for Anne and Margot stands at the site of the former Bergen-Belsen camp, where they died in 1945. Their remains are believed to be in an unmarked mass grave.

No one knows for sure how the police found out they were there. On September 3, 1944, the Frank family was sent to a camp called Auschwitz in Poland. Anne's father was separated from his family. He never saw them again.

Anne, Margot, and their mother were forced to do hard labor. It was cold, wet, and there was not enough food. Anne and Margot were moved to a camp in Germany called Bergen-Belsen. Edith Frank died in January 1945. Anne and Margot got sick with **typhus**. They died in February 1945. Their father was the only person from the annex to survive the Holocaust. The Holocaust is the mass murder of Jews by the Nazis in the 1940s.

At the Anne Frank House Museum, visitors can tour the Franks' hiding place and learn more about Anne's life.

Anne's Legacy

Anne's diary was found and given to her father when he returned from the camps. He read how Anne dreamed of becoming a writer. He published her diary in June 1947. Millions of people around the world have read *The Diary of a Young Girl*. It has been translated into about 70 different languages.

Anne Frank House

Today, the building where Anne hid is a museum called the Anne Frank House. People from around the world visit it each year. They learn about Anne's life and legacy.

Anne continues to inspire readers all over the world through the words of her remarkable diary.

Anne lives on through the words she wrote in that secret annex. Her diary helps readers understand what life was like for Jews during the Holocaust. Readers are reminded of the high cost of hatred. But Anne's words also demonstrate the importance of showing love and strength even in the worst of times.

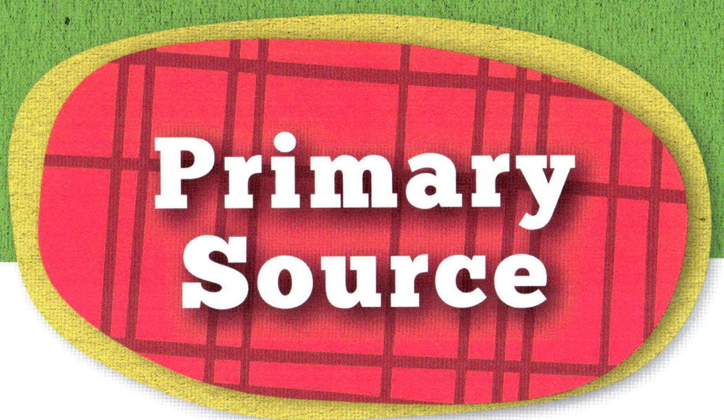

Eva Schloss's family was also captured by the Nazis. She and her mother survived. Several years after the war, Eva's mother married Otto Frank. Eva wrote:

> I could not see why I should be put into prison or why, at the age of fifteen, I was such an undesirable person because I was Jewish. It was all a senseless persecution.

Source: Eva Schloss. *Eva's Story: A Survivor's Tale by the Stepsister of Anne Frank.* W. B. Eerdmans Pub. Co., 2010.

What's the Big Idea?

Read this quote carefully. What is its main idea? Explain how the main idea is supported by details.

Timeline

1929
Anne Frank is born on June 12 in Frankfurt, Germany.

1933
Hitler gains control of Germany in January. Due to rising hatred of Jews, Otto Frank moves to Amsterdam, the Netherlands. He is later joined by his family.

1940
The Nazis invade the Netherlands on May 10.

1942

On June 12, Anne receives a diary for her thirteenth birthday. On July 6, Anne and her family go into hiding.

1945

Anne dies of typhus in a Nazi camp in February.

1944

The Nazis raid the secret annex on August 4 and arrest everyone inside.

1947

Anne's diary is published.

Glossary

annex
a building attached to a larger main building

ethnic
having to do with a group of people who share a culture, religion, or language and live within a larger national group

Nazi Party
a German political party from 1920 to 1945

rights
things all people should be granted no matter who they are or where they come from, such as equality, fairness, and respect

synagogues
Jewish houses of worship

typhus
an infectious disease caused by lice, mites, and fleas in unclean places

Online Resources

To learn more about Anne Frank, visit our free resource websites below.

Visit **abdocorelibrary.com** or scan this QR code for free Common Core resources for teachers and students, including vetted activities, multimedia, and booklinks, for deeper subject comprehension.

Visit **abdobooklinks.com** or scan this QR code for free additional online weblinks for further learning. These links are routinely monitored and updated to provide the most current information available.

Learn More

Bassier, Emma. *Anne Frank*. Abdo, 2020.

Herman, Gail. *What Was the Holocaust?* Penguin Workshop, 2018.

Index

About the Author

Heather C. Hudak has written hundreds of kids' books on all kinds of topics. She loves to travel when she's not writing. Heather has visited about 60 countries. She has been to Anne's hometown in Germany and also to the Anne Frank House in the Netherlands.